Rawan Fuller

DIARY
OF A
MINECRAFT
WOLF

BOOKS KID

TABLE OF CONTENTS

Day 1

"Spot! Sit down!"

"Spot! Come here!"

"Spot! Roll over!"

Do you know how boring it gets being told what to do all day?

My name is Spot and that's a really stupid name for a wolf. When I was living with my pack, my name was Renaldo Algernon Magnificent, but when I was a pup, I wandered too far from my pack and I got picked up by a Minecraftian who took me away with him.

He thought he was doing me a favor, showing me a world of adventure. He probably thought that I'd been abandoned by my mother and needed someone to look after me, but I can look after myself. I have sharp teeth and I'm not stupid.

That's half the problem. Because I can learn tricks really quickly, Jim, the Minecraftian decided he'd teach me to do all sorts of silly things. Want a wolf who can count up to three by barking? I'm your guy. Think it's the funniest thing in the world to see a wolf who can dance? Stick on some music and watch me boogie. Need a wolf to weave in and out of poles? I'll weave like I've never woven before.

So you've probably heard of me, since I'm the most famous wolf in the whole of Minecraftia. I'm one half of Jim and His Incredible Wolf, Spot. The half that does all the work but doesn't get any money for it. Jim seems to think that all I need is a bone and a pork chop and I'm happy.

To be fair, bones and pork chops do make me happy.

Still, it doesn't seem like this is the sort of life a wolf should be leading. I should be out in the wilderness, fighting zombies and racing with the pack.

Every night, I look at the moon and howl for what I've left behind.

Day 2

"OK, Spot. We're going to work on some more of your tricks today. We're going to be at another village shortly and I want to make sure that we're going to impress them. I'm running a bit low on funds, so we need to put on a really good show if we want to make lots of money."

I don't know why we don't do what most Minecraftians do when they want money – mine for it. That is why this place is called Minecraftia, after all! At the very least, we could fight our way through a few monsters and explore temples and fortresses, looking for hidden treasure. That would be fun!

But no. Jim has to insist on making me do stupid tricks to impress stupid villagers for stupid money and I'm sick of it.

"Right. Let's start with opening the door. I've built a little frame for you to practice with. Remember, people always like it when we start the show with you making an entrance."

I padded round to the other side of the door and waited for my cue.

"Spot! Where are you Spot?"

Sighing, I reached up a paw and pushed the door open, walking through to what was usually loud applause from the waiting villagers.

"Shut the door behind you, Spot!"

I turned around and nudged the door shut with my nose.

Jim started to run me through our repertoire of tricks, switching up the order in which he asked me to do things, just to keep the show exciting. He always said that if people never saw the same show twice, they'd keep on coming back for more and we do perform to packed audiences every night wherever we go.

We never stay too long in one place either, so people can't wait for us to come back.

At last, Jim said we were done for the day and I sank down next to the campfire as he cooked my pork chop.

"You know, it was a lucky day when I found you, Spot," he told me. "You're going to keep me rich for the rest of my days. Who wants to waste all their time mining when you can just get a wolf to do the hard work for you?"

I rolled my eyes. Yes, he certainly was lucky when he found me.

Day 3

"There it is, Spot. The village that's going to be our home for the next few days."

I looked down at the village in the valley below us. It didn't look like anything particularly exciting, but Jim said that it was on a main road that went through a number of important towns in Minecraftia, so there was going to be plenty of passing Minecraftians to come and see our show.

He led the way down into the village as I trotted obediently alongside him. "Now, Spot. Time to start generating some interest."

Jim pulled out some posters from his bag and I held them in place with my paws while he stuck them to the sides of buildings.

"Hey! You! You can't do that!" An angry villager came rushing out of his house, protesting at Jim putting a poster up on his wall.

"Oh, I'm terribly sorry sir." Jim was well used to this, so he instantly turned on the charm, smiling pleasantly at the villager as he handed him the poster we'd been sticking. "I was just trying to advertise our show: Jim and his Incredible Wolf, Spot."

The villager looked at me. I looked at him.

"He doesn't look very incredible," he sneered.

"Ah, but you wait until you see him on stage. He comes alive! Don't you Spot?"

"Woof." I nodded my head, knowing just how much this impressed people. How stupid is that? A wolf nods and the crowd goes wild. No wonder Jim makes so much money out of me.

"So he can talk. What else can he do?"

"I think a better question to ask would be what can't he do?! My Spot is really incredible. You've never seen anything like it."

The villager folded his arms and sniffed, clearly not convinced.

"Tell you what. I'll give you a free ticket to our show tomorrow night. If you don't like what you see, then I'll give you your money back. You can't say fairer than that, can you?"

The villager frowned as he tried to figure out what he'd get back on a free ticket, while Jim smiled and pressed a piece of paper into his hand that would get him into the show.

"Bring all of your friends with you!" Jim called over his shoulder as we moved on to put more posters up, knowing full well that the villager wouldn't just bring his friends – he'd bring his family and everyone he knew.

By the time we'd finished working our way around town, it was clear that we were going to be performing to a full house tomorrow night, just like we always did.

Day 4

"Ladies and gentlemen, boys and girls, good evening and welcome to the show!" The crowd clapped politely, but they weren't exactly going wild – yet. Still, if the lukewarm reaction bothered Jim, he didn't let it show as he went on with his introduction.

"My name is Jim and I've got an incredible wolf I'd like to introduce to you, but he seems to have gone missing. Can you help me find him, boys and girls?"

"Don't know," mumbled the crowd.

"I said – can you help me find him, boys and girls?"

Jim mouthed the word 'yes' and made encouraging movements with his arms and eventually he got a few people in the audience to cry "yes."

"All right, so after three, I want you all to shout with me 'Spot, where are you?' One... two... three... Spot, where are you?"

I waited on the other side of the door, knowing that I wasn't meant to enter just yet.

"Oh dear, boys and girls." Jim shook his head. "I don't think that was loud enough. Spot didn't hear you. Let's try again. Spot, where are you?"

I nudged the door with my nose, just enough to make it move, but not so much that it actually opened.

"One more time, everybody. Spot, where are you?"

That was my cue. I pushed open the door, walked into the middle of the room and walked straight back out again.

"Oh dear. I think he's shy. Are you shy, Spot?"

I poked my head around the door and nodded.

"We're not going to hurt you, are we boys and girls?"

"No!" yelled the children, more excited now that they'd seen an actual wolf.

I trotted out into the room and sat down in front of Jim.

"Do you want to see Spot do some tricks?"

"Yes!" Even the grown-ups joined in, calling out to see me do some tricks. Jim took me through some of our most popular commands, making me dance around the stage, going up to a villager and offering them a paw as if I wanted them to dance with me, finding objects hidden among the audience and counting how many children were lined up on stage.

Finally, on a nod from Jim, I went to his bag and pulled out a blanket, going over to a corner, curling up and pulling the blanket over me.

"I think that's Spot telling us it's time to go. We'll be back tomorrow with another show, folks, so if you liked what you saw tonight, make sure you come back again for a show that's even bigger and better!"

Day 5

"Did you enjoy our show last night?"

This time, the reaction to Jim's introduction couldn't have been better. Everyone whooped and cheered as they waited to see what we had in store for them tonight.

"Well for our first trick, I'm going to need a volunteer from the audience. Who thinks they can run faster than a wolf?"

Everybody put their hand up. Jim selected the smallest child he could find. "You, sir. What's your name?"

"Colin."

"Well, Colin, we've got a little obstacle course laid out for you. You'll need to jump over this hurdle, crawl under this one, and then go through the tunnel at the end. Whoever leaves the tunnel first is the winner. Got it?"

Colin nodded as we both took our places at the starting line.

"On your mark... get set... go!"

As I'd been trained, I paced it carefully so that Colin felt as though he had a chance of winning. We were running side by side until we hit the tunnel. As soon as I was out of sight, I raced ahead, shooting out of the other end long before Colin crawled out.

"Never mind, Colin. Have a sweet."

Colin took his seat as Jim turned to the audience. "So who else thinks they've got what it takes to beat Spot?"

This time, he chose a man, someone who looked really athletic and desperate to beat me. As we lined up at the starting line, the man beat his chest, getting cheers of support from the crowd.

He didn't stand a chance.

I ran five races that night, each time going faster than I had before, winning each race without any trouble.

By the time the night was over, I was crowned the ultimate racing champion after beating three Minecraftians in a long and complicated obstacle race.

"Well, folks, Spot is getting a bit tired now, so we're calling it a night, but come back tomorrow for our last show. You know you're going to love it!"

I watched Jim counting up all his emeralds as he tossed me my nightly bone. It really didn't seem fair that he was getting rich while I had to do all the hard work. I'd like to see him win five obstacle races in one night!

Day 6

I'm so glad that it's the final show tomorrow. Jim gave me the day off, said it was to create more interest in what we're going to do at the last performance, but I'm just glad of the rest. It's very tiring having to make the villagers happy.

We had a visit today from the villager leader, who wanted to know whether I was being well treated.

"Oh, you don't have to worry about Spot," Jim assured him. "Spot loves performing, don't you, Spot?"

Actually, I hate it. I hate being at the center of attention while I do all those dumb things. Wolves weren't meant to dance. The villagers love it, but standing on my hind legs for so long makes them sore and the music hurts my ears.

"Do you mind if I see where Spot stays when he's not on stage?" asked the leader.

"Of course, not." Jim was all smiles as he took the village leader on a tour of our camp, showing him my little bed and blanket. "Spot gets a pork chop and a bone every night. He's very well looked after. You don't have to worry about him."

"Some of the villagers said that he looked really miserable during last night's show."

"Spot? Miserable?" Jim laughed. "Never! I guess they're just not used to what a wolf is supposed to look like. If Spot didn't like performing, then he wouldn't do it. It's that simple. You can't make a wolf do something he doesn't want to do."

"Very well. I'm satisfied that you're taking good care of Spot. I'll tell the other villagers that there's nothing to worry about."

The village leader left and Jim lost his smile. "Interfering busybody," he muttered. "It's none of his business how I look after you. You're my wolf and you have been since you were a pup. He needs to keep his nose out of my affairs."

I kept quiet. Jim might not be happy that the leader came to visit, but he'd given me an idea.

Day 7

The room was packed full of villagers and traveling Minecraftians, all desperate to see what we were going to do for our final show. They were certainly going to get the surprise of their life when they saw what I had in mind.

"Ladies and gentlemen, boys and girls, I cannot tell you how happy Spot and I are that you're here with us for our last night in your beautiful village. You've made us both feel very welcome and we're going to be very sorry to leave you. We hope that our final show makes you happy and is our little way of saying thank you for your kindness over the past few days. Spot insisted on getting you a little present, and he's going to bring it out on stage for you now. Spot! Come on out!"

I ignored him, staying right where I was, curled up in my basket.

"This is very odd. Spot must be feeling a bit shy tonight. Come on out, Spot!"

I didn't move.

"Boys and girls, you're going to have to help me. Call him with me – come on out, Spot!"

Not even all the boys and girls of the village were enough to make me move from my comfortable cushion.

Jim stormed off stage and out to where I was waiting. "What are you doing?" he hissed through clenched teeth. "Get on out to the stage. The audience is waiting for you."

I yawned and stretched, but didn't move.

OUCH! Jim kicked me!

"Now get out there or there's more of that to come."

I growled as Jim shoved a bunch of flowers in my mouth and led me out on stage.

"Here he is, everybody. Say hello to Spot!"

"Hello, Spot!"

I walked around, dropping a flower in front of members of the audience until I didn't have any left to give.

"Spot has got a song to sing to you, now, haven't you, Spot?"

I glared at him.

Jim lifted his foot, miming a kick, so I threw my head back and howled a few bars of Minecraftia, the best place to live, the national Minecraftian anthem. It had taken me ages to learn how to sing it. It's a very difficult tune.

By the time I'd finished, the audience had joined in with me and I could see a few wiping tears from their eyes. Minecraftians are very proud of their world.

"Now, who'd like to play a game of soccer?"

Jim picked out a few children from the audience, while I obediently trotted over to the goal he'd set up. I spent the next ten minutes knocking balls away until a child finally managed to get one past me. (I let him.)

Jim gave the child a pumpkin pie as a prize and then it was on to the grand finale, where Jim and I did a dance together. He used to do high kicks with me and really put a lot of effort in, but over the years, he's become lazy, so us dancing together really is just Jim shuffling about in the middle of the room while I do all sorts of fancy moves around him.

At last the show was over and I couldn't wait to get out of there, but Jim wasn't going to let me go to bed.

"What was that?" he demanded. "How dare you disobey my commands? We have a show to put on and our audience expects us to be incredible each and every time. That's why the show is called Jim and his INCREDIBLE wolf! I don't want you ever to try and pull a stunt like that again. Try it and I'll show you exactly what happens to those who go against me. You're not the first wolf I've trained. There are plenty of others who'd love to be where you are now, with a nice hot meal every night and the chance to travel the world."

Somehow, I doubted that there were many wolves out there desperate to be Jim's sidekick.

"Anyway, you can forget about any bones or pork chops tonight. Wolves who don't work, don't get paid. You can do without for tonight. Now get back in your basket – go on!"

I snarled at him, but slunk away to my bed. If Jim wasn't careful, he'd be without the wolf who made him so much money.

Day 8

I listened to Jim counting all his diamonds as we made our way down the road, out of the village and to the next town.

"Even with you being silly, we still did very well at that place. Very well indeed. Keep this up and I might give you an extra rabbit once a month. Not too much – I don't want to spoil you – but you do deserve a bit of a reward for your efforts. Just make sure that you don't pull any more stupid stunts like you did on that last night, all right?"

I said nothing. I'm a wolf. We don't talk to Minecraftians – or at least that's what people think. The truth is that we can speak Minecraftian, but we don't bother most of the time. It's not like Minecraftian conversations are all that interesting.

"Did you see that shelter I built?"

"Yes. It must have taken you ages."

"I would have finished it sooner, but I had to keep fighting the zombies that spawned."

"Oh no! Not zombies! I hate zombies!"

Boring!

Wolves are all about the thrill of the chase, working together for the good of the pack. We're too busy having fun to build anything.

I would never speak Minecraftian to Jim anyway. Can you imagine what would happen if he found out that I could talk? He'd make me do twice as many shows and if I was lucky, I might get a bit of beef steak once in a while.

No, Jim is never going to find out that I'm a talking wolf.

Day 9

"You know, I've always dreamed of retiring young," Jim told me as we continued our journey to the next village. "I'd build my ideal shelter high in the hills with a view over the plains and I'd get an iron golem to bring me food every day while I sun bathed. If I get bored, I'll just count all my emeralds and diamonds. That will never get boring. I had no idea how I was going to get enough resources to be able to do that until I found you.

"I really hit the jackpot with you. You know, it was very difficult luring you away from your pack. I never thought I'd get you to leave your mom's side, but in the end, the smell of pork chop was just too much for you to resist. I knew there was money in a performing wolf, but I had no idea that you were going to be as talented as you are. You pick tricks up faster than any other wolf I've ever seen. That's why we're so famous – no other wolf can do the things you do."

He carried on talking, but I wasn't paying attention any more. He hadn't just found me, lost in the forest. He'd deliberately wolfnapped me!

If Jim knew that I could understand every word he said, he never would have told me the truth about how I came to work for him. As it is, there's no way that I can stay with Jim, not when I know that my family's out there, wondering where I am. I always thought that something had happened to them, which was why I was abandoned. Now that I know that Jim stole me, I have to get away and back home.

Wherever home is.

Day 10

"All right, Spot. We're going to be at the next village soon, so let's go over some tricks to practice. I don't want you to get stage fright again. You made me look really stupid when you stopped performing and I'm not having it again. Let's start with balancing a treat."

He put a piece of meat on my nose and I shifted so the meat fell off without Jim seeing me move.

Jim picked it up and put it back on my nose again. I moved again. It dropped again.

I had to bite my tongue to stop laughing after I'd done this for the sixth time, as Jim became more and more frustrated with the meat not balancing.

"Fine. We'll leave that one for the moment, then. Let's do the commando crawl. Down, Spot!"

I got down on my belly and crawled along as if I were sneaking up on a skeleton. I hate doing it. A wolf should only crawl if it's hunting for something, not because Jim is telling a story on stage and I'm acting it out.

"Good, good. Let's do the freeze game."

He turned his back on me and I crept up behind him. When he turned round, I stopped moving, staying so still you'd think I was a statue.

He turned his back on me again and I started moving forward again until Jim spun round, my cue to stop dead in my tracks.

At last, I caught up with him and I jumped up on his back. It was so tempting to sink my teeth into him and just run away, but I didn't want to do anything until I could figure out how to find my family again. Minecraftia is a big place and Jim and I have spent many years on the road. I needed to pick my moment carefully before I made my move.

Day 11

"Here we are, Spot. This is one of the biggest Minecraftian villages around. I've got high hopes for us making a lot of money here. I might even be able to take a holiday when we've finished here. It's been a long time since I've had a holiday and I deserve a break."

Good job he didn't see me roll my eyes. Still, I suppose that carrying all those diamonds and emeralds must be tiring work. Yes, I'm being sarcastic. From where I'm standing, Jim's life is nothing but one non-stop holiday.

"I've decided that we deserve a treat. We're going to stay at the guest house," Jim said. "Well, I'm going to stay at the guest house, that is. You'll have to sleep in the stables. They don't like wolves in the bedrooms. You leave too much fur all over the place."

Great. The stables. I hate sleeping in the stables. The horses smell of, well, horse, and the straw tickles my nose and makes me sneeze.

Jim led me to a large building. "You wait here," he ordered. "I'm going to go in and book my room. Sit, Spot. Stay!"

I sat down while he went inside, looking around at the passing villagers. This seemed just like every other village I'd ever been in, even if there were a few more people.

"Look at the cute doggy, mom!" A little kid dragged his mother over towards me.

"No, Sebastian! Don't touch it! That's not a dog, it's a wolf!"

"A wolf? Cool!" Sebastian looked at me. "I want to pet it. It doesn't look like it's going to bite me."

"It's a wild animal, Sebastian. You can't trust it. Its owner is nowhere around."

I decided that it was time for a trick or two, so I stood up and did a somersault.

"Did you see that, mom? That was amazing!"

"I did." His mother's eyes were wide and I could tell that I'd impressed her.

I put one paw out and shook it up and down. The kid quickly took the hint and reached out to take my paw so we could shake hello.

"It's a friendly wolf, mom!" cried the boy.

"It's a friendly, performing wolf." Jim came out of the guest house to stand by me. "He's going to be doing some shows here later in the week. You should come along."

"Oh, no, we couldn't. I'm sorry, but we don't have the money for things like shows," apologized the mom.

"Money?" Jim waved her objections aside. "I couldn't possibly let a lovely family like you pay for your tickets. Here you are – two front row tickets for opening night. All I ask is that you tell all your friends about Spot and how talented he is. Do we have a deal?"

"That's very kind of you, Mr…"

"Jim. Call me Jim. And this is my incredible wolf, Spot."

"Jim, well, I'm afraid that we can't accept these. It's very kind of you, but it wouldn't be right."

"Oh mom, can't we go to the show? Please? Please?"

Sebastian looked at his mom, begging her to let him see my show.

"All right then," she sighed eventually. "If you really want to. Thank you, Jim. We shall see you at your show."

"Look forward to it." Jim smiled as the two villagers walked off. "They're lucky to get these tickets. I've been talking to my contact in the town and we're looking at sold out shows every night. Get ready to be busy, Spot. You're going to be the wolf everyone is talking about!"

Day 12

I had a terrible night's sleep in the stables. The horse smell was even worse than I remembered and I couldn't get comfortable on the straw. I spent all night walking round and round in a circle, trying to make a bed that I could lie down in, but just when I thought I had somewhere nice to lie, a bit of straw would stick up and poke into me.

Not what you need when you're supposed to be entertaining people.

When the day broke, I yawned, stretched and went outside to explore the town a bit. First thing in the morning, it was still quiet and I enjoyed the peace as I wandered about, taking in all the new sights and smells.

I caught a glimpse of what looked like Jim hurrying down a narrow alley between some houses. What would he be doing up so early? It wasn't like him to get up with the sun, so I followed after to see if it was really Jim I'd seen or someone who looked like him.

As I made my way down the alley, I heard Jim's voice. It was definitely him.

"If you're interested in buying my wolf, I'm going to have to warn you that he won't come cheap. He knows more tricks than any other wolf in Minecraftia. That wolf is going to keep me in diamonds for the rest of my life."

"I'm sure that we can come to some arrangement. I have plenty of diamonds to pay for the right wolf. How does this look for starters?"

I edged closer, poking my nose round the side of the building to see what the mysterious stranger was offering. I almost yelped when I saw the enormous chest filled to the brim with diamonds.

"It will do." I knew Jim well enough to know how excited these diamonds would be making him, but he was always good at hiding his feelings when money was involved.

"Well, bring your wolf to me at the end of the week and there'll be five chests just like this one waiting for you. You can keep these diamonds as a sign of good will in the meantime."

"I haven't agreed to your terms yet," Jim pointed out.

"You will," grinned the stranger before turning and walking off.

Jim was going to sell me! As if I was nothing more than a piece of meat or enchanted weapon. Well, if Jim thought that he was going to retire early because of me, he had another thing coming.

Day 13

"Spot, this is going to be our best week ever!" Jim couldn't stop smiling all the way through our final rehearsal before the show. "Tickets are selling faster than ever and that's after I put the prices up. I need you to make the audience gasp, cheer, and raise the roof! There's a lot of money riding on this and you can't let me down."

I looked at Jim, knowing the real reason why he was so happy. If I put on a good performance, he was getting more diamonds than he'd know what to do with. Of course he was smiling all the time.

"Now for the first show, I want you to go round and collect up all the glasses from the table before cleaning up any mess from the floor. That's bound to get a laugh."

Yay. I get to pick up garbage.

"Then I want you to play a short tune on the piano. Nobody will have seen that before."

I hated playing the piano. Sitting on my back legs got really sore after a while and Jim always shouted at me afterwards if I got a note wrong.

As Jim went through his plans for the show, I realized just how much I hated my life. I wasn't cut out to be a show wolf.

I was going to have to make some big changes and Jim wasn't going to like them.

Day 14

"Ladies and gentlemen, boys and girls, put your hands together and welcome Spot to the stage!"

The sound of the audience cheering was so loud that you could probably hear it in the Nether. Well, I didn't care how loud they were. I wasn't going on stage tonight. Not for anything.

"Spot seems a little shy. Let's give him another round of applause."

I buried my head in the straw, not caring if it made me sneeze. I'd had enough of Jim and his shows.

"I'm sorry, ladies and gentlemen. I'm going to have to go and see what's taking Spot so long. I'll be back in a moment."

Jim burst into the stables, his face as black as thunder. "Just what do you think you're doing, Spot? There's a room full of people out there all waiting to see you. They've paid good money to see you. This is no way to treat them."

I shrugged. What did I care about how much they'd paid?

Jim pulled out a big stick. "I don't care how much of a star you think you are, you're not going to ruin things for me. Get out there right now or I'll make you sorry you were ever born."

WHAM! He brought the stick down hard right next to my head. I could feel a rush of air from where the stick had moved and I yelped, jumping to my feet.

"Next time I won't miss," growled Jim. "Now get out there, wolf, and do exactly what you're supposed to do."

My tail between my legs, I slunk out on stage. I could see Sebastian and his mom sitting right in the middle of the front row and the little boy waved at me when he saw me walk onto the stage.

I lifted a paw to wave back, which gave me an idea. I pretended to limp on the stage.

"What's wrong with him? He's hurt! Somebody help that poor animal!"

I grinned to myself as Jim hurried out on stage behind me. "There's nothing wrong with him. It's just one of his tricks," he reassured the audience. "Show them, Spot. Dance for me!"

I tried to jump up onto my back legs, but I dropped down again, yelping as if it had really hurt.

I could see Jim was getting mad, which was exactly what I wanted.

"What have you done to him? Boo! Boo!" The audience was getting restless and in desperation Jim rushed to my side.

"I don't know what game you think you're playing, but it better stop fast or you'll be in serious trouble."

I yelped, edging away from him as if I was scared. If I'm honest, I was a bit scared of what he was going to do after the show.

Out of the corner of my eye, I noticed the man who'd offered Jim diamonds for me shake his head, get up, and walk out of the room.

"No! Wait!" protested Jim. "There's nothing wrong with Spot. He's just being silly. Come on, Spot. Get up!"

"That's enough." Sebastian's mother got up and crossed over to stand by my side. "This wolf has clearly been badly treated by you. Who knows what injuries he's suffered at your hands? I suggest you leave now before we make you leave."

"That's right! Leave! Leave!" The crowd started chanting and Jim knew when he was beaten.

He turned tail and rushed out of the room before things turned ugly.

"Come on, Spot. You're coming home with me." I looked up and saw Sebastian smiling down on me. Weakly, I licked his hand to say thank you.

Day 15

Nobody has seen Jim since he ran out last night. Apparently, all his things are gone from his room and nobody knows where he's gone.

Good. If I never see him again, I won't be sorry.

Sebastian has been doing his best to make sure that I'm comfortable. No sleeping in stables now that I'm staying with him! He's made me a little nest at the bottom of his bed with my very own cushions. I could just lie there all day.

"There. You're safe now. The nasty man is never going to come back," he soothed as he gently stroked my head.

"I know," I whispered.

"You can talk?" Sebastian gasped.

I gulped. I'd forgotten where I was for a moment. What should I do? I could pretend that I hadn't said a word. Sebastian was just a kid and everyone knew that you couldn't believe anything a kid told you.

But he'd been so kind to me from the moment he'd met me and I was tired of having to hide my true nature from everyone.

"I can talk," I finally said.

"Wow! You really are incredible! Why didn't you ever talk in the shows you did?"

"I didn't want to let Jim know. He wasn't very nice to me."

"I know. Mom said that he beat you black and blue which is why you were limping last night."

"Ah." If a wolf could blush, I'd be bright red. "Jim didn't hurt me last night. But he said he was going to and he was about to sell me to someone, and who knows what they were going to do to me? It was the only way I could think of to make Jim look bad and get away."

"Oh." Sebastian thought for a moment. "That's really clever. Maybe I should try that the next time I don't want to go to school."

"Or maybe you shouldn't," I warned him. "You don't want your mom to think that I'm a bad influence, do you? She might send me away."

"I don't want you to go!" Sebastian threw his arms around me and hugged me tightly. "I won't do anything like that. I promise."

"Good."

"So what did Jim do that was so terrible, then? I always thought it would be really cool to be a performer. You get to travel the world and everywhere you go, people love you."

"Yes, well, that's not quite how it was for me." I told Sebastian all about how Jim had stolen me from my family and made me work for very little reward while he kept all the money. "So now I want to see if I can find my family again," I finished.

"Can I help?" offered Sebastian. "We've been studying wolves in school so maybe I can help figure out where your family lives."

"That would be great." I smiled at Sebastian. "I need you to promise me one thing though."

"Anything."

"You can't tell anyone that I can talk. Jim isn't the only person out there who wants to use me to make money. This is our little secret."

"I won't tell anyone," promised Sebastian solemnly.

I think I'd found my first friend.

Day 16

Sebastian came home from school with a huge book in his backpack. "This is my textbook about wolves," he explained, dragging it out and putting it on his desk with a thud. "I thought it would be a good place to start looking for where your family might be from. Maybe you might recognize a picture."

"Good idea."

Sebastian started flicking through the pages, but nothing looked familiar.

"I'm sorry, Sebastian," I sighed. "None of this looks like anywhere I know. I was only a cub when Jim snatched me. I don't really remember much of what it was like to live with the pack."

"That's all right, Spot. Let's get a map of Minecraftia and mark the possible places where your family might be. Then we can figure out a way to check them all out."

I didn't like to tell Sebastian that his plan might take years. Having spent so long touring with Jim, I knew just how big Minecraftia was. Instead, I simply said "that could work."

"Great!" Sebastian jumped up and grabbed another book from the shelf. Opening it up, I could see that it had lots of maps of different biomes in Minecraftia. "OK, Spot. Let's start making a list of locations."

"All right. But first, could you do me a favor?"

"Anything you like."

"Call me by my real name – Renaldo. Spot was Jim's name for me and the sooner I forget about it, the better."

"Of course… Renaldo."

Day 17

Sebastian was so excited about helping me find my family that he forgot to do his homework. His mom was not pleased.

"If that wolf is going to be a bad influence on you, we're going to have to find another home for him," she warned.

"But mom, that's exactly what we're trying to do. I'm helping Renaldo find his family again."

"Renaldo? I thought his name was Spot?"

"He told me- I mean, I thought that Renaldo suited him a lot better. Spot's a stupid name for a wolf."

"And Renaldo is better?"

"I like it," protested Sebastian. "It makes him sound like he's someone special and he is someone special. He's my friend."

"Well friends don't stop you from doing your homework, so you'd better get upstairs and start on your math or there'll be trouble."

"Yes mom."

"Don't worry, Sebastian," I whispered as he made his way to his room. "I'm really good at math. I'll help you with your homework and we'll be done in no time."

"Awesome!"

Sebastian's homework was really easy and between the two of us, we had it finished in record time.

"I want you to do my homework with me every day!" laughed Sebastian as he shut his last textbook. "It was so much fun and you're such a good teacher. I never understood how to do division until you explained it to me."

"You're a good student," I replied modestly. "It's easy to teach when someone listens."

"Well we're all done now, so we can get on with the hunt for your family."

He opened up the atlas marked with all the different Minecraftian locations where wolves were found. There were packs all over the world. Finding my family was going to be impossible.

"Think, Renaldo. Is there anything you can remember about your old home?"

I wrinkled up my snout as I tried to recall what my childhood home was like. "There were lots of trees," I said finally.

"OK, trees." Sebastian made a note on a piece of paper, sticking his tongue out as he concentrated. "What else? Was it hot or cold?"

"It was quite warm I think."

"Good, good, that helps. What about the trees? Do you remember anything about what they looked like?"

I thought some more. "They were different from the trees around here," I said at last.

"Did they look like these?" Sebastian showed me a picture.

"Yes! That's exactly what they look like!"

"Spruce trees," nodded Sebastian. "I think you come from the Taiga."

"The Taiga!" The word sounded strange but familiar. "Yes! I think you're right!"

"Then we know where we need to start looking," smiled Sebastian.

Day 18

It's really weird not having to do shows every day and move from town to town. This is the first time in my life I've ever been able to stay in one place and build a home. I'm really liking it.

The only thing is that now that I know that I'm from the Taiga, I want to go back there to see if I can find my family. I hate the idea of leaving Sebastian behind, but I need to see my family again, let them know that I'm all right.

I don't know what to do.

Day 19

"Sebastian! Renaldo! Could you come down here for a moment, please?"

Sebastian and I looked at each other. We'd been right in the middle of plotting our route to the Taiga and I was getting even more excited at the thought that I might see my family again.

We went downstairs and I stopped in my tracks at what I saw.

The man who'd offered Jim diamonds for me was standing next to Sebastian's mom.

"This is Mort. He's an expert in wolves. He's come to take Renaldo to live with his other wolves."

"No! You can't!" Sebastian threw his arms around my neck. "I won't let you take him. We're going to find his family."

"Now, Sebastian. Don't be like that. I know you want what's best for Renaldo and he needs to be with other wolves, not living in a village. Mort knows all about looking after wolves. He'll make sure that Renaldo has a good life. He'll take care of him properly."

I growled and shook my head backing away.

"It's all right, Mrs. Miggins." Mort stepped forward, putting a hand out in a calming gesture. "It's understandable that the boy has become attached to the wolf. He's a fine specimen. A very fine specimen indeed." Mort smiled and it looked as though his teeth had been sharpened. I knew that there was no way I was going anywhere with him. I had a horrible feeling that I wouldn't last very long if I did.

"See, mom. Renaldo doesn't want to go with him. You can't make him." Sebastian stood in front of me, his arms outstretched to protect me.

"Move out of the way, Sebastian," his mom ordered. "You're being silly now. When we rescued Renaldo from that nasty showman, I never meant for him to stay with us forever. We were always going to have to find him a new home and this is perfect."

"Come on, kid." Mort tried to keep smiling, but it was more of a grimace now. "You don't seriously think you can have a wolf living in your bedroom, do you?"

He lunged forward, knocking Sebastian out of the way and making a grab for me.

"Noooooo!" I howled.

Everyone froze.

"Did that wolf just… talk?" Sebastian's mom fainted.

"That settles it. You're mine, wolf." Mort went for me again.

Sebastian and I looked at each other. There was nothing else we could do. We ran out of the house as fast as we could.

Day 20

"You shouldn't have come with me," I said to Sebastian as we made our way down the road that led out of the plains. "You belong at home with your mom. She'll be worried."

"I know, but you're my friend and I need to make sure that you're safe. Mom will understand when I explain things to her. We needed to get you away from that Mort guy. I didn't like him at all."

"He tried to buy me from Jim before," I told Sebastian. "I didn't like him then either. I don't know what he planned to do with me, but I couldn't hang around to find out. Still, we're far enough away from the village now that I'll be safe from him. You could go back to your mom. I'll be fine by myself."

"I'm not leaving your side until we've found your family," Sebastian replied loyally. "Besides, do you know how to get to the Taiga?"

"No," I admitted. "But you don't either."

"That's where you're wrong," beamed Sebastian. He pulled a crumpled piece of paper out of his pocket. "I tore this out of the textbook before I gave it back to school. It's a map that shows the way to the Taiga."

He flattened the paper out and we both crowded round, trying to plot our route.

"So we're here." Sebastian pointed to a place on the map. "And the Taiga is over here." He ran his finger up the page to show where we needed to go. "It'll take us a few days, but it looks pretty straightforward."

I nodded, trying to pretend that I knew what he was pointing at when really it just looked like a whole heap of squiggles.

Sebastian laughed. "You don't know how to read a map, do you?"

I shrugged.

"It's all right. Neither did I until the teacher showed us. It's very simple. These lines are roads. These different colors show what the land is like. The blue bits are water. We're on this road here. We need to stay on it until we reach this junction and then we should be able to cut across the plains."

"That looks very easy. We should be there in five minutes!"

Sebastian laughed. "It'll take a little longer than that. The map is tiny compared to the real world. But I don't think we'll get lost."

Neither of us asked how we were going to find my family in the vast expanse of the Taiga.

Day 21

"I'm hungry," complained Sebastian. "I haven't had anything to eat all day. I didn't get any sleep last night either. I don't understand how animals can sleep outside all the time. It's cold and miserable."

"I'm sorry, Sebastian." This was exactly why I didn't want him to come with me to find my pack. Humans just weren't good at dealing with being on the road. I was used to it after my years with Jim, but Sebastian was just a villager kid. This was a whole new world for him and I knew he was going to find it tough. "I can go and see if I can get some meat for us if you like."

"That would be good. Thank you, Renaldo." He slumped down against a tree and I laughed.

"Look up, Sebastian."

He did as he was told and gasped at what he saw. "Apples!"

"That should keep you going until I bring back some meat."

Sebastian picked an apple and sat there, happily munching while I slunk off into the undergrowth, hoping to find a nice juicy rabbit.

My ears pricked up at the sound of rustling in the bushes. Crouching low, I crawled forward, trying to stay as quiet as possible so whatever it was wouldn't notice me approach.

Slowly, ever so slowly, I poked my nose out through the leaves. I had to stifle a gasp when I saw what was there. It was no rabbit, that's for sure. Mort was trying to make a fire for his camp!

I edged back until I thought I was out of earshot and then raced back to where I'd left Sebastian.

"That was quick," he said. "Did you catch anything?"

"No." I shook my head. "But we have to get out of here. Mort is just over there. If we stay here, he'll catch us for sure."

"Mort?" Sebastian scrambled to his feet. "But how could he have found us?"

"I guess he came down the same road we did. There's only one road from your village to the Taiga you said. It's not that hard to find us if we're all going the same way."

"Well we can't stay on the road," said Sebastian, his rumbling tummy completely forgotten about in the face of this new challenge. "We'll have to cut over the hills. It might be hard work, but it's the only way to keep you safe.

Still, at least we have the map. That will help us figure out the way to go to stay on the right track."

Day 22

There was no sign of Mort. Leaving the road seemed to have kept us safe and although Sebastian must have found it tough climbing up and down hills, he didn't complain.

He's a good kid.

"So where to now?" I asked when we stopped for a break.

Sebastian looked at the map. "There are mountains over there. I don't think Mort will follow us through them, but it's going to be cold and it's a lot of climbing."

I looked at what Sebastian was wearing, a simple villager's robe. It wasn't really going to help much in the snow.

"What are our other options?"

"We can keep going the way we are and hit the plains. We'll be exposed though – if Mort is around, he'll be able to see us from a long way off. Or we head off this way and get back on the road. Mort has probably gone on ahead of us by now, so if we stay alert, we can stay safe."

None of our choices were great.

"Which way is going to be the fastest?"

"I think probably the plains. If we use the road, we'll have to be slow so that we don't catch up with Mort. Although it's easy for him to spot us on the plains, we'll also be able to see him, which will give us time to run away. If we move as quickly as we can, we can be through the plains and onto the Taiga in no time."

"All right. The plains it is."

I would have preferred going through the mountains, but I had to think of Sebastian. We'd come too far for me to send him home by himself now, and there was no way he'd cope in the mountains.

We'd just have to move fast and hope that Mort didn't see us.

Day 23

"What's that on the horizon?" Sebastian pointed at something in the distance. My heart leapt. Had he spotted some wolves?

I looked over to where he was pointing. A plume of smoke curled up into the sky.

"That's not good," I muttered.

"Why?"

"If we're lucky, it's just some Minecraftians camping out."

"And if we're not?"

"Mort has guessed that we left the road and he's on his way to catch us."

After all the trouble he'd had to go to to track us down, I didn't think he'd be in a good mood if he caught us and I didn't want to hang around and see what Mort's temper was like. Something told me that it would be a lot worse than Jim's.

"We'd better hurry, then."

Sebastian did his best, but villagers aren't as fast as wolves and he soon fell behind. I raced back to him. "Jump on my back," I ordered.

"Are you sure? I don't want to hurt you."

"I'm stronger than I look," I reassured him. "Just make sure you hold on tight. I don't want you to fall off and hurt yourself."

"I won't." Sebastian scrambled up on my back, grabbing handfuls of my fur to steady himself.

I started running, the extra weight from the villager kid barely slowing me down in my desperation to get away from Mort. I had no idea what that man had planned for me, but I hadn't liked him from the moment I'd first seen him and I didn't want to find out what he would do to Sebastian if he caught up with us. He might want a wolf, but I didn't think he needed a villager kid hanging around.

"Over there! Go over there!" Sebastian nudged me with his knees to try and get me to go to the right. "I think I can see a Minecraftian camp. We can get them to protect us against Mort."

I changed direction, sprinting as fast as I could. I was going so fast that by the time I realized what had happened, it was too late.

We'd run straight into the middle of Mort's camp.

Day 24

"You really are an awful lot of trouble for one little wolf." Mort paced up and down in front of where he had me tied up. "If it wasn't for the fact that you're going to make me a fortune, I'd kill you right now. Luckily for me, I knew exactly what you were from the moment I saw you, even if that Jim was too stupid to spot it. It's the black moon behind your ear that gives you away as one of the rare talking wolves. All your pack are the same, but usually you stick together and it's impossible to catch any of you. I don't know how that Jim managed to trap you, but his loss is my gain – and I didn't even have to pay him all the money I promised. Yes, today is my lucky day all right."

I glared at him, too angry to speak.

"As for you, my little friend." Mort kneeled in front of Sebastian who was tied up right next to me. "I'm afraid you're of no use to me."

"So just let him go," I demanded.

"Oh I couldn't possibly do that," chuckled Mort. "I'd love to, but I can't risk him coming back and trying to set you free. But don't worry. I'm not completely heartless. When we move on, I'll leave him here with some food. I'm sure a passing Minecraftian will untie him and he can go back home."

"And if they don't?"

Mort shrugged. "A resourceful villager kid like him is bound to be able to sort something out. Whatever. It's not my problem."

"Why are you doing this?" cried Sebastian. "Why can't you just let us go?"

"I told you," Mort said. "This wolf is going to make me a fortune. You can never have too many diamonds in this world. You have no idea how long I've waited to find someone like Spot."

"My name is Renaldo," I snarled.

"Your name is whatever I say it is," sneered Mort. "If you think it was hard doing what Jim told you to do, you haven't seen anything yet. Your life is about to get a whole lot tougher."

"Let us go. Please, just let us go." Sebastian began to cry.

"Oh do shut up," Mort snapped.

"Why don't you let them both go?"

The three of us turned and couldn't believe what we saw. An entire pack of wolves had surrounded the camp and were all growling at Mort. My pack had found us!

Day 25

"How did you find us? How did you even know we were there? What did you do to Mort? Where are we going now?"

"Slow down, Renaldo," laughed Salvador, the leader of the pack, as we ambled along the road back towards Sebastian's village. "One question at a time."

"How did you find us? We hadn't reached the Taiga yet. I thought we still had a few days of walking before we reached you."

"The pack is always on the move," Salvador replied. "We usually stay within the Taiga, but something told me that we needed to go a little further out this time. Our pack has the ability to sense when one of our own is in danger, so I had a feeling that somebody was in trouble, but all the pack was together, so we hurried to see who was calling to us. I couldn't believe it when I saw you tied up like that. You've been lost for so long that we had almost given up hope of finding you again. What happened?"

"I was stolen by a showman," I said bitterly. "I've been touring all over Minecraftia, doing stupid tricks for the humans. I thought I was going to have to do that forever."

"Tricks, eh?"

"Yes. Like this." I did a somersault before rising up onto my hind legs, taking Sebastian's hands and dancing around with him.

The other wolves clapped and laughed. "That's awesome!"

"It's nothing, really," I blushed.

"You know, a lot of the wolves would love to see your show," Salvador told me. "There's a big difference between doing tricks for peanuts and taking charge of your own destiny to do shows the way you want to. You're clearly a natural performer. Maybe you could put together something just for the pack."

"Maybe." The truth was that there were things I'd liked about being on stage. I liked making people smile and laugh. If I could do that for my pack without having to deal with someone like Jim, maybe I could still do my shows.

"So what happened to Mort?" asked Sebastian.

"He's been taken to the nearest village where he'll be locked up for a very long time. Mort is a wanted man, you know. He's been trading in unusual animals, finding rare creatures and then selling them on to people who enjoy eating special food that most people can't afford to buy."

I gasped. Mort had planned to cook me?

"Don't worry, Renaldo. He can't hurt you now. You're with your family and we're going to keep you safe."

Family. A word that held so much meaning and something I never thought I'd find.

Day 26

I had so much to learn about being part of a pack. All the other wolves seemed to know what the pack was thinking, but I struggled to work with them.

The pack all went hunting, but I soon got left behind and I double back to sit with Sebastian, who was waiting at the camp.

"Is everything all right, Renaldo?" he asked. "You're back early."

"It's fine," I sighed.

"Come on, Renaldo. I know you better than that. What's wrong?"

"It's just that I don't feel as though I'll ever fit into the pack. I'm too used to being on my own."

"Give it time," Sebastian advised. "It must be strange for all of you. Your pack didn't think they'd ever see you again and I know how much they must have missed you. I've watched the other wolves and they're all so happy to have you back with them. You'll figure out your place in the pack soon enough."

"I never thought I'd miss Jim, but it was a lot of fun when we were together on stage. Most of the time. On the days when he promised me an extra rabbit."

"So why don't we pretend we've got a stage?" suggested Sebastian. "Salvador did say that the wolves would like to see your show. We can practice a few tricks together and perform to the other wolves before I go home. It would be like our thank you for rescuing us from Mort."

"That's a brilliant idea!" I gasped. "We can do all my favorite tricks. But not dancing. I always hated dancing."

"Well why don't you tell me to dance?" said Sebastian.

"You're a genius! Nobody has ever seen a wolf tell a villager what to do."

"So that's settled. We can practice when we camp for the night and do the show the last night before we get back to my village."

"Sounds like a plan." I didn't want to think about saying goodbye to Sebastian. That kid had changed my life, and the pack was taking him back home to make sure that he was safe. It wasn't going to be the same without him around.

Day 27

The show was coming along nicely. It was a lot more fun working with Sebastian than Jim. Sebastian didn't boss me about. He asked me what tricks I wanted to do and then listened to me so that we could work out the best possible show. The other wolves were going to love what we had planned.

We were making good time back to Sebastian's village. The wolves took turns letting Sebastian ride on their back so we could run faster, and since we didn't have to worry about avoiding Mort, it didn't take long before we were back in the familiar surroundings of the hills around Sebastian's village.

"Not long now before we get you back home," smiled Salvador to Sebastian. I tried to smile as well, but I hated the thought of leaving him. "Your mom must have been very worried about you. Speaking of moms, your mom is back in the Taiga with the other half of the pack, Renaldo. I sent a couple of wolves back to tell her that we'd found you again. She never gave up hope. She always said that one day you'd come home. I'm glad that I'm able to be the one to take you back."

My mom! All I remembered about her was the smell of her fur, someone warm to cuddle up to at night, while she smiled at me, telling me how much she loved me. It would be amazing to be back by her side.

"We should be at the village tomorrow and then we can head home."

"Before you take me back, Renaldo and I have a little surprise for you," said Sebastian. "We've put together a show to say thank you for rescuing us."

"A show by Sebastian and his incredible wolf, Renaldo? That will be amazing! When we set up camp tomorrow we'll clear out some space for you. The wolves will love seeing what you can do."

Day 28

My heart raced. I'd never felt this nervous before a show before, but then I'd never performed for my pack. What would they think of what I was about to do? Would they think I was a bad wolf because I was useless at hunting, but I could weave in and out of Sebastian's legs?

The wolves gathered round, howling in welcome as Sebastian went out in front of them.

"Ladies and gentlemen, boys and girls, welcome to our show. I am extremely proud to present the incredible Renaldo!"

The wolves cheered, but I stayed off stage, just as we'd rehearsed.

"Oh dear. It looks as though Renaldo is a little bit shy. Let's call him. Renaldo!"

"Renaldo!" cried all the wolves.

I walked backwards out onto the stage area, covering my eyes.

"Renaldo?"

I jumped, pretending that Sebastian had startled me, doing a somersault to land facing him.

The wolves gasped at my acrobatics, but they hadn't seen anything yet.

Sebastian and I went through everything we'd practiced. It was the best show I'd ever done. We did magic tricks, making a rabbit appear from behind Sebastian's ear, to the amazement of the audience. I told Sebastian to dance and he did a silly little routine, wiggling his bottom at the audience to make them laugh.

Finally, Sebastian and I sang a song together, my voice rising over his in perfect harmony as we sang a tune we'd written together, just for the wolves: My pack, my family, my friends.

When we were done, all the wolves rose to their feet, howling and stamping on the floor to create a loud noise in celebration.

"That was the best show I've ever seen!" cried Salvador. "You two are incredible together!"

"I know," I smiled at Sebastian. "We make a good team together."

"It seems such a shame to split the pair of you up, but we're at the village now and Sebastian needs to go back to his mom."

"Can't I stay with you for just one more night?" pleaded Sebastian. "One more night won't make any difference, and I don't know when I'll see Renaldo again. I'm sure my mom won't mind."

"I don't know." Salvador looked at us, thinking. "I know how much Renaldo's mom has missed him and I'm sure yours will be worried sick. Still, it is getting late. I suppose we could let you stay with us for one more night and take you back home first thing in the morning."

"Thanks, Salvador."

Sebastian snuggled up next to me when we settled down for the night. "You're my best friend," he told me. "All the other kids at school are going to be so jealous when I tell them about our adventures. None of them have a talking wolf for a best friend."

"None of the wolves have a villager kid for a best friend either," I replied. "I'm the luckiest wolf in the world."

Day 29

"Sebastian! Oh, Sebastian, where have you been? I've been so worried about you!" Sebastian's mom came rushing out of their house as Sebastian and I walked into the village, the whole pack right behind.

"I had to save Renaldo," he explained. "Mort was going to sell him to someone so they could eat him!"

"Eat a wolf? Don't be ridiculous."

"It's true," said Salvador.

Sebastian's mom looked at him and fainted.

"Come on, wolves. Let's get her inside and comfortable."

The wolves worked together to carry Sebastian's mom into his house and we all gathered around her, fanning at her to bring her back round. At last, her eyelids fluttered and she opened her eyes.

She looked around and when she saw Sebastian, she smiled weakly. "Oh Sebastian. I had a terrible dream. I dreamt you'd run away with a whole pack of wolves and then when you came back again, the wolves talked to me!"

"That wasn't a dream, mom," said Sebastian. "Renaldo and his pack can talk."

"It's true, we can," I nodded.

Sebastian's mom screamed.

"You don't have to be afraid of us," I reassured her. "Sebastian saved my life. It's true. Mort was a butcher who dealt in rare meat. When you agreed to give me to him, he was going to get countless diamonds and emeralds from some rich person who wanted to know what talking wolf meat tastes like. Sebastian helped me find my pack. Without him, I wouldn't be alive. He's a hero."

"I just did what anyone else would do," said Sebastian modestly. "I know that mom would never have listened to Mort if she knew what he had planned."

"Of course not!" exclaimed his mom. "I didn't rescue you from that nasty Jim person just to see you slaughtered. I'm sorry, Renaldo."

"That's all right. You didn't know."

"Mom..." Sebastian began. "I wanted to ask you something. Renaldo and I have been working on a show together and it's really good. Could I go with Renaldo and his pack to take our show around the world?"

"Absolutely not!" retorted his mom. Sebastian's face fell. She grinned. "Not unless I can come with you, that is. I always wanted to know what it was like out in Minecraftia."

Renaldo and I looked at each other, hardly daring to believe what we were hearing. Sebastian could come with the pack. We weren't going to be separated after all!

Day 30

As we left the village behind, I couldn't believe how much my life had changed. I was free of Jim and I had a best friend and my pack. I had everything a wolf could want.

All I needed to do was meet my mom and life would be complete.

"Who's that up ahead?" Sebastian pointed to some wolves coming towards us on the road.

Salvador squinted. "Renaldo, I think you're about to be a very happy wolf. The scouts I sent have brought your mom back to meet us."

My mom?

I started racing towards the coming wolves and as I did, I saw one of them break away and come running up to meet me.

"Renaldo! My Renaldo!"

As we met in the middle of the road, I realized that I would have recognized my mom anywhere. She looked just like me, right down to the strange moon marking behind her ear. We barked and jumped around, giving each other wolf kisses and touching noses.

"Let me look at you," said mom at last, stepping back. "You've gotten so big! Oh my baby cub. I'm so proud of you. I always knew you'd find your way back to me."

"Mom, I'd like you to meet someone." I moved aside to let Sebastian come forward. "This is my best friend, Sebastian. If it wasn't for him, I'd have ended up on someone's dinner plate."

"Thank you, Sebastian. If there's ever anything the pack can do for you, you only have to ask."

"I already have everything I need," beamed Sebastian. "Salvador has agreed that me and my mom can join you on the road so that Renaldo can do his show with me."

"His show?"

"That's right." I stood up proudly. "I'm Renaldo, the Incredible Wolf and Sebastian is my Minecraftian."

Sebastian put his arm around me and mom stepped forward to join the hug, as the other wolves all gathered round in one big, pack hug.

"Come on, everyone, let's get moving," cried Salvador. "We need to take Renaldo back to the Taiga. There's still the rest of the pack waiting to meet him."

All the wolves howled. "Climb on my back, Sebastian," I cried, as another wolf came up behind his mom, nudging her so that she fell on his back.

"Let's go!"

The wolves started running, heading towards our new life, happy and free.

Printed in Great Britain
by Amazon